Every Decision Counts

8 Lessons I Wish They Taught Me in School

Tre' Gammage

EVERY DECISION COUNTS. Copyright © 2019 by Tre' Gammage

All rights reserved. Except as permitted under the U.S. Copyright Act of 1976, no part of this publication may be reproduced in any form or by any means without the prior written consent of the author. The only exception is brief quotes used in reviews. Thank you for your support of the author's rights.

For copyright inquiries, please direct your request to:

tre@tregammage.com

Cover Design: Rickie Sarratt of Casting Crowns Media

Interior Design: B.O.Y. Enterprises, Inc.

Printed in the United States of America

ISBN: 978-1-7338051-6-2

Table of Contents

Introduction

A Letter to Readers

Part 1 Failing Got Me Started

Chapter 1 Failing Got Me Started

Chapter 2 Only Quality People

Chapter 3 Make New Mistakes

Part 2 Hold Nothing Back

Chapter 4 Hold Nothing Back

Chapter 5 Every Decision Counts

Chapter 6 Praising Insecurities

Part 3 Released Expectations

Chapter 7 Released Expectations

Chapter 8 What's Growing in Your Garden

Introduction

Growing up I got to live two different lifestyles at the same time. My parents were never married but dad always came by to visit, and never missed a football or baseball game.

I say two different lifestyles because I lived with my Mom until I was 15 and was an only child until I was 12 when my brothers Saeed, then two years later Zane was born. My mom is the most loving, supportive, and ambitious women I know. We didn't have the most money growing up, we moved 11 different times by the time I finished college. There were some Christmas mornings that someone else or an organization had to buy the presents or clothes. And if we were to ask my Mom for twenty dollars, it might be the last until she gets paid.

But we never knew it, my brothers and I had a great child hood because she treated us with love. When we could, we would travel as often as possible. I learned about African American heritage and about loving God. When my Dad would pick me up in his smooth red Cadillac Escalade and we drove to the North side of town, it was a completely different lifestyle.

He was a defense attorney and our family name Gammage meant a lot to the city. My grandfather grew up picking cotton in Ita Bena, Mississippi before migrating to South Bend, Indiana where he became a well-known entrepreneur and servant leader. My Dad built on that legacy by becoming the third black Judge in the 200-year history of St. Joseph County Indiana.

When I went to go visit my Dad's house with my siblings, Austin, Delorean, and Valencia, there was a different type of pride in the house. My Dad would teach us about taxes, investments, scholarships and push us to be the best version of ourselves. When I asked him for twenty dollars, he would pull out a wad of cash and hand me some money. It was about hard work, giving back, and taking care of your business. See what I mean with two different lifestyles?

Because of my experience growing up in these different lifestyles, I got to meet a lot of people, and more importantly learn from their successes and failures. As it turns out you can turn all of the challenges, pains, and misfortunes that life throws at you into motivation, opportunity and success. Through my experience, I've realized that in life there are some situations that happen around you, some that happen to you and other situations that you were born into. While you can't change what's already happened, you can decide what comes next.

The purpose of this book is to equip you, our young adults, with the self-awareness, principles, and skills you need to turn every obstacle into a platform for opportunity.

A Letter to Readers

Dear Readers,

At the end of the day, this book is to help you stay ahead of the curve. There are eight lessons. Each one is designed to help you prepare for what's coming next. Anybody can learn from their own mistakes, but the great ones learn from other people's mistakes. Yeah, I said it, people make mistakes, but losing doesn't have to be an option. You either win or you learn. Also, each of the eight lessons you are about to grow through is about real people, real stories, real situations. I don't want you to just read through this book, I want it to change your life.

I've made each chapter interactive. While you read, you will have to do the work, practice, or assignment that's a part of each chapter. Yes, you are going to be challenged to ask and answer some questions that you may not have answers to, yet. If you want help or want to invite me to your school to talk about Every Decision Counts while walking you through the steps just let me know.

Go to tregammage.com, Facebook, Instagram, or LinkedIn to contact me about working with you to make every decision count.

Part 1: Failing Got Me Started

It's ok to be wrong just try not to make the same mistake twice. Failing got me started is a journey through failing, homelessness, and big mistakes. In this case, failing was the best thing that could have happened. It's not about failing, it's about how you bounce back.

Chapter 1
Failing Got Me Started

Most people look at failure as a weakness. In fact, failure is classified as a weakness, shortcoming, or flaw. But you don't have to think about failing in the same way. Fail = First Attempt in Learning. In this lesson, you'll explore failure and how you can start to fail forward.

Let's be real, in life you are going to lose a lot more than you win. Think about it, a Hall of Fame Baseball Player hits the ball 3 times out of every 10 at bat. The GOAT Michael Jordan missed every other shot making him a 50% career shooter. When is the last time you lost? It could have been a small bet with your siblings, a not so hot test score, or some kind of video game or athletic competition. You've experienced the joy of victory, the satisfaction of defeating all of the obstacles in your way, the pride that comes along with a good W, but failing probably isn't on your list of things to do.

Just to be clear the Webster Dictionary definition of fail is to be unsuccessful in achieving one's goal. Losing is the worst. Often, you start complaining, and blaming others for your loss, become irritated, stressed, and begging to run it back. It's hard being a good loser. I'm not bringing up failure because that's what I want you to do. Instead, I'd like to show you that failure is how you get started.

Are you familiar with a grandfather clock? They are usually tall clocks and at the bottom there's a weight that swings from left to right, ticking and tocking. The most famous grandfather clock I know is in Beauty and the Beast. The clock was friends with the candle. If you've never seen it, Google "Beauty and the Beast grandfather clock" you'll see what I'm talking about. That piece of the clock that ticks and tocks is what keeps the clock on time, it's called a pendulum. It swings left and right all day. The rhythm of the clock is what keeps time moving forward. You can think about this pendulum on the grandfather clock the same way you think about success and failure. The tick doesn't exist without the tock. If you don't lose, victory doesn't taste so sweet. Success doesn't happen without failing along the way.

Take the Kid President for example. Do you remember him? Robby Novak, he's the little boy on YouTube wearing a suit giving the world a pep talk. If you forgot, his YouTube channel is called Soul Pancake, or you can Google 'kid president'. Well, the Kid President suffers from Osteogenesis imperfecta, a disease that makes his bones brittle. He broke 70 bones and had 13 surgeries by the time he was 9 years old! Even still, he was nothing but positive. He was in a cast from waist down, bed ridden in the hospital, yet he was still inspiring, so his family decided to start recording him giving speeches. At first, they were just for family, but once the videos were uploaded to YouTube, 'The Kid President' became an international star. He failed first, rather his body failed him. It wasn't a choice to break all those bones and be such a fragile young man. This is the hand life gave him, so he ran with it.

Let's talk about a better way to think about failure.

Fail = First Attempt In Learning

Before you move forward, take a moment and think about your First Attempt In Learning. It's ok if it takes some time to think about your examples. Especially if it's your first time thinking about failure in a positive way. If you need help, work with a partner, friend, classmate or teacher that can help you think about what you've learned.

Practice – Talk with two of your favorite people about their experience with failure or google two of your favorite people and include the word 'fail' after their name.

Example: Michael Jordan Fail, Beyoncé Fail, or Barack Obama fail

Ask someone you look up to the following 3 questions. Write their response in your own words. (1 – 2 sentences)

1. Has there ever been a time that you've learned from failing?

_____
_____

2. What does losing/failing teach you about who you are?

_____
_____

3. How can you turn failure into motivation to succeed?

_____
_____

Describe three times you've experienced a failure that helped you learn in the long run.

1. _____
_____

2. _____
_____

3. _____
_____

Failing forward

So, you've explored your own defeats, seen some famous failures, and reached out to people close to you about how Failing is a First Attempt In Learning.

If you haven't, go back and do the work!

Are you ready for the next step? It's not good enough to talk about it, you've got to be about it. You are familiar with the true meaning of failing. But what does that mean for you? How can you use this information today?

Three easy ways to turn failure into a learning opportunity:

1. Make your bed– Sounds silly right? Making your bed is a key to success.

I used to hate making the bed in the morning. I'm just going to jump back in and mess it up when I get back home. But making your bed isn't about being clean, it's about doing something right. When you make your bed in the morning, no matter how bad your day was, you get to come home to something you did right! I know it's pretty easy, and really simple. So why not? You can fail a test, lose a game, get in trouble, lose something special and still end your day with something you can be proud of because you took the time and did it right.

2. Brush your teeth. You can keep laughing but bad breath is a great way to start off on the wrong foot. If you don't brush your teeth you lose as soon as you open your mouth.

This goes hand in hand with making your bed. The little things matter the most. There's an old quote by Ralph Waldo Emerson that says, "The things that are easy to do are easier not to do. But if you do the thing, you will have the power."

Start your day off with two easy victories, make your bed, and brush your teeth.

3. Raise your hand – Yes literally raise your hand in class and raise your hand in life. Let's think about your classroom first. The teacher asks the whole class a question, but only a few people are willing to answer. Everybody else doesn't want to be wrong. Either you don't want to sound stupid answering the question wrong, or you don't want your class to laugh at you for asking a question when you aren't sure.

Don't allow your fear to keep you from your First Attempt In Learning. Show up just like the man in the arena the 26th President of the United States, Theodore Roosevelt, spoke of in his opening speech.

"It's not the critic (person judging you) who counts, the one who points out how the strong stumble and where things went wrong. The credit belongs to those willing to step into the arena, striving, coming up short time after time, because without failure there is no effort. Those willing to commit to doing the work know that the best-case scenario is a triumphant victory and at worst if he fails, at least he fails while daring greatly. Not worrying about those who don't know victory or defeat." (to see the full quote, look up 'the man in the arena')

Next time you are in class, don't be the critic who talks about everybody who tries. Be the man or woman in the arena who is willing to put in the effort.

Chapter 2

Only Quality People

Growing up isn't all about the materialistic things. It's about the people you surround yourself with and the relationships you form. Social media has made it easy to let conflict and drama slip into your life. That's why it's so important to surround yourself with 'only quality people'.

Random question: Who is in your corner? List the 5 people that are closest to you.

1. _____
2. _____
3. _____
4. _____
5. _____

Crabs in a Barrel

Are all five of these friends or family members quality people? In other words, do these people make you better or do they hold you back? It's a really important question because all your friends and family members may not share the same mentality (way of thinking). There are some people who think, "Well if I can't have it, neither can you." If they get in trouble, they are going to get you in trouble too. If they are sad, they will try to make you sad. If they don't like somebody, you can't be their friend either. We call this a crab in a barrel mentality. When a fisherman goes crabbing, all the crabs they catch are placed in a barrel so none of the crabs can escape. Even though all of the crabs hate being in the barrel, and are all working hard to escape, the fisherman doesn't even need to put a lid on the barrel. When one crab decides they want more out of their crustacean life and starts to find her way out of the barrel, the rest of the crabs pull her back down. The crabs have the mentality of, "if I can't have it, neither can you."

Let's step away from the metaphor for a minute and think about how this mentality might show up in the real world, at your house, in your class, or relationships.

Here are a few examples of what a crab mentality looks like:

- If I can't have it neither can you

Watch out for people in your life who want everyone else to fail.

- You feel good about yourself, but talk bad about everybody else

You only want to hear the good things people have to say about you. When someone tells you the truth about an area you can improve in, you don't want to hear it.

On the other hand. you only see the mistakes in other people and never point out the good. Some people call it joking, some say roasting… either way there's never a positive comment about somebody else.

- When your friends do well, you start to panic

This is just pure envy, jealousy and bitterness. People with a crab mentality get nervous when the people around them start to make progress. That's when they start pulling you down, using harsh words, or unkind actions because they are feeling insecure.

- Treating friends like competitors

You might start to notice that some of your friends never think about 'we' or 'us'. In their head it's all about 'me'. These people are everywhere, the hooper/baller that doesn't care about losing as long as his stats look good… they would rather see the team lose than win without being the star player. This friend wants all the credit but doesn't do well cooperating with others.

- Spending more time talking about people rather than discussing ideas and solutions

Since friends in a crab mentality are competitors, most of his time is spent talking bad about other people. Why? Because you don't want to see anybody become better than you.

- They will never admit to their crab mentality

This is the hardest part, even if you have this mentality and are reading about yourself now, you probably won't admit it.

Experience with a crab mentality

Reflect on three (3) personal experiences or examples of a crab in a barrel mentality. Include at least one instance when you or someone you know were holding other people back.

1. _____
_____
_____

2. _____
_____
_____

3. _____
_____
_____

A Shark Mindset is a Growth Mindset

Opposite of a crab mentality is a Shark Mindset. Did you know sharks can't swim backwards? And if they stop moving, they will die? Sharks only move forward. When you have a shark mindset, you have a growth mindset. You believe that you can be a better version of yourself. Failure to you is a temporary setback. When someone else gets a good grade, or win's a game, you are inspired to improve your effort. You don't mind making mistakes because you realize you either win or learn.

Sharks live with a Growth Mindset. They believe the following:

- Intelligence and talents can be developed
- Effort is the key to success
- Mistakes are a part of learning
- Failure is an opportunity to grow
- Failure is temporary
- Challenges should be embraced
- Feedback should be welcomed
- Another person's success is inspirational

Crabs live with a Fixed Mindset. They believe the following:

- Intelligence and talent are fixed, they can't change
- Effort is fruitless
- Failure defines who you are
- Flaws should be hidden
- Change should be avoided
- Feedback should be ignored
- Feedback is personal criticism
- The success of others feels threatening

Only Quality People

Surround yourself with Only Quality People. It's too easy to talk trash. The top five people in your life should be people that want to push you to be a better version of yourself, that want you to grow and tell you about yourself when you start acting up.

You become like the five people you spend your time with. Look back to the five (5) people in your corner. Are these the people that are supposed to be there? Be honest with yourself.

Let's write down the top 5 Quality People in your life

1. _____

2. _____

3. _____

4. _____

5. _____

Did your list change? If not, good job! You are surrounded by sharks and you are always moving forward. If there's a new list, I appreciate your honesty. You don't have to kick your old friends to the curb, but you can let them read this chapter or have a conversation about Crabs vs Sharks.

Here's a secret for you, if you aren't sure where to find more quality people find a book about your favorite person or watch some videos on YouTube about them. Your brain doesn't know the difference between what's in your head and what's in front of your face. Sometimes the best help comes from the people you've never met.

Chapter 3

Make New Mistakes

Privilege is what you are born into, race, gender, wealth, education. When you are born on the wrong side of privilege, you are often born into a sink or swim lifestyle. This means you must make life changing decisions all the time just to survive. Making so many crucial decisions at such a young age can often lead to mistakes. It's ok to make mistakes, just try not to make the same mistake twice. Here's how you can learn from your mistakes.

Every day you face barriers that you can push past by knowing what you are capable of. It starts with doing the little things right and learning from the people around you. It's important to learn from other people's mistakes and from your own.

I have a friend named Robert who trains athletes to perform at the highest levels. It's amazing to see his rise because he started in the streets. Robert lived the life that rappers talk about.

"You've got to be aware to be in the streets, to be a good judge of character and recognize the people who want to see you shine and the ones that don't." – Robert Torres

He learned to recognize the routes that people take. One route can lead to jail, another can lead to scholarships. In Robert's case, he chose the streets at an early age, living in different shelter homes, eating donated food, and carrying a gun for protection.

When the people around you aren't making it out of a bad situation you have to make the blueprint yourself or end up as a statistic. (sink or swim) Robert found himself in a situation where he was going to sink. Facing more than 10 years of federal jail time for his affiliation with gangs and drugs, Robert was given a second chance when the charges were dropped.

Ask yourself this question:

Is this the best version of yourself?

The answer was no for Robert, so he made a change and started making straight A's in school. By the time high school graduation came around Robert worked to become the Valedictorian (#1 ranked student in class) and presented a graduation speech about Making new mistakes.

Making New Mistakes

You don't run out of tries in life. When you make a mistake, you have an opportunity to grow bigger, badder, and stronger. You are going to hear NO a lot more than you hear YES. The ratio is approximately 17:1 which means you are going to hear no 17 times for every 1 yes.

If you want the result you have to put in the work. The results you earn are always going to teach you something about yourself. Even when the outcome is poor, you are learning something. Once you learn from your mistake you can let it go and move on.

Learn from your mistakes

I'm 100% sure you are going to make a whole lot of mistakes in school and life. I remember being in fourth grade and making a mistake with a substitute teacher. The class had a running joke about her because she always talked about her cats, she walked really slow, and looked like Godzilla. I decided I wanted to get in on the joke, when she asked me a question I responded with, "Yes, Mrs. Godzilla". It was funny in the moment, but it wasn't funny when I was sent to the office and got suspended for two days. My mistake was trying to fit in and keep up with my classmates. But they weren't the one's that got sent home, I was.

As I got older, the mistakes kept coming. One of the biggest lessons I learned was when I earned my scholarship to play football at Miami (Oh) University. First of all, yes there is a school called Miami located in Oxford, Ohio named after the Myamia Indians. When I got my full ride scholarship, I thought I made it. It felt like the rest of my time in college would automatically be a success. Sike! That's not how it works, I didn't put in the effort necessary to be the best. I relied on my past success when nobody cared about what I did in high school.

As a result, I rode the bench for two years, and didn't get to start a game until my senior year of college (we'll talk more about this in chapter 5). The lesson? You have to earn every step.

Tre' Gammage

These mistakes have helped me be the person I am today. What mistakes have you made recently? What kind of lesson did you take away from it?

1. _____

2. _____

3. _____

Part 2 Hold Nothing Back

Life can be captured in the fleeting in between moments. Once you see someone living their dream it makes you want to be a part of theirs or go get your own. Hold nothing back in your pursuit of purpose.

Tre' Gammage

Chapter 4

Hold Nothing Back

Instead of getting lucky in your success, do it on purpose. Nothing big is going to happen for you unless you do the little things. If you work to get just 1% better each day, in one year's time, you'll be 3x the person you are today! Who do you have to be to achieve your wildest dreams?

I've always worked hard but I've never prepared for success. Instead of just working hard, find something you are chasing. My friend Justin Maust started off helping his brother's dream come true, and then he started living his own! Nothing big happens unless you do the little things.

When you are given a dream, you have a responsibility to make it your reality. Would you believe me if I told you the wealthiest place on the planet is a graveyard? Yup a graveyard is where the cure for cancer lies, the idea that can end world hunger, and the solution to bad cafeteria food. All of these lay buried in a graveyard. People died filled with potential because they were too scared or didn't put in the work to make their dream come true. Nothing big in life happens unless you are willing to do the little things.

To be clear, I'm not saying your dream is going to be easy. I'm saying when it comes to the pursuit of your dreams, your purpose, and success… HOLD NOTHING BACK! Take the chance to go get what you want.

When you see someone living their dream it makes you want to be a part of that dream or start to live your own. Live your dream.

The Compound Effect

Growing up, sports were my jam. I started with baseball in kindergarten, and then football in 3rd grade. I tried basketball, but I was awful. I was cut from my 7th grade team and decided to play in a city league. We lost every single game that year, but in the last game of the season with time winding down and the score tied up the ball found its way to my hands. I wanted to pass it, but the time kept ticking 3….2… SHOOT! 1…. AIR BALL!!!!!!

That was the end of my basketball career. Baseball was cool, but I couldn't hit a curveball so that was over too. Football it is! See ball, get ball. Run and hit. I can handle this. My talent alone led me through middle school and into high school. However, varsity football in high school was another level. The guys were so strong and so big. Growing up I was always naturally bigger and faster than everybody but that didn't fly in high school.

After my junior season playing middle linebacker my Dad and I were reviewing the season. I said, "You know Dad everybody thinks I had a pretty good season, but I don't think I deserve all this recognition."

Dad replied, "Well Tre, I think you are right. I thought you sucked. All I remember is you running up to make a tackle and sliding right by the ball carrier."

Laugh if you want, but it hurt, because it was true. This is also one of my OQPs (only quality people), helping me learn from my mistakes. Something had to change if wanted to live out my dream of playing Division 1 College Football.

Over the next 6 months I committed to being the hardest working person in the school. Every day, once the bell rang to go home, I went straight to the weight room. Sometimes it was locked so I ripped it open. In the morning, I'd eat my breakfast and pack two sandwiches. I ate one before lunch and the other after lunch. During the real lunch period, I would eat my lunch and find a girl who had free lunch so I could eat hers too. My dream was on the line, so I held nothing back. By the time the next season started I was a whole new player with 30 new pounds of muscle, super speed and a mission to be the best.

People used to call me 'Bevo latte, got more head than he got body'. All that changed my final year, because I put in the work. The secret was building skill instead of relying on talent. Talents are what you are born with. Some people are talented singers, artists, musicians or athletes. Greatness comes when you turn the talent you are born with into a skill.

What are your top 3 skills? Ask 10 friends what you are the best at and see what you get.

Ex. Question to ask: What am I the best at?

1. _____

2. _____

3. _____

The compound effect is the ripple effect from the choices you make daily. They can be good or bad choices that you make every day. At first it seems like they don't matter, but over time they can take you places you could never imagine.

To compound your talent into skills so you can be the best version of yourself, focus on getting 1% better each day. That's all… just 1%. You can be a .5% better reader, .25% better friend, and .25% better at one of your talents. 1% better each day means that in 365 days you will be 37x better. Can you imagine who you can be? You aren't just adding 1% each day you are multiplying 1% each day. The growth is exponential like an algebra equation.

Victory Loves Preparation

These victories don't come on accident, you have to work to set yourself up for success. You've heard a part of my story through football and you know your top three talents.

What are three habits or ways you can get 1% better every day at your three talents?

Examples

Talent: Basketball

Three ways to improve: 1) Dribble for 10 minutes a day. 2) Shoot 10 free throws a day. 3) Do 10 pushups and 10 sit ups a day.

Talent: Reading

Three ways to improve: 1) Read 10 pages a day. 2) Read a more challenging book. 3) Have conversations about what you've read.

Talent: Talking when I'm not supposed to

Three ways to improve: 1) Give compliments to 3 people each day. 2) Have on task conversations in class. 3) Think before speaking.

Tre' Gammage

My commitment to get 1% better each day

Talent: _____

Three ways to get better.

1. _____
2. _____
3. _____

Talent: _____

Three ways to get better:

1. _____
2. _____
3. _____

Talent: _____

Three ways to get better:

1. _____
2. _____
3. _____

Chapter 5

Every Decision Counts

The moment it feels like your decisions matter the least is when they really matter the most. Life is all about you and it's not about you. It's all about you because only you control the decisions you make each day. At the same time, it's not about you because your decisions impact other people too.

The only way to win is by doing. Everyone wants the end result but not many people are willing to put in the work. Life is difficult and you don't get to change what you were born into, what happened to you, or the experiences that you have already had. However, you can decide how to use them.

In college I played football at Miami (Oh) University. No not the University of Miami Hurricanes. The Miami University Redhawks. Our school was formed in 1809 when Florida was still owned by Spain. Anyway, it was the best of times and it was the worst of times. We lost a lot of games, 21 in a row to be exact. It was the longest active losing streak in the country back in 2014.

My experience started off just like I dreamed all my life. This beautiful red brick campus, fresh cut green grass, and all those girls! It was a dream come true, until it wasn't. In high school I was the best player on my team, but when I got to college that changed. Everyone was bigger, faster and stronger than me. Some of my teammates had kids, others had beards. I wasn't ready.

For the first two years of college I rode the bench, I didn't receive one second of playing time, even though I still had to do all of the work. Here's what my schedule looked like:

5:30 AM – 6:30 AM Weightlifting twice a week

8:00 AM – 1:00 PM Go to classes

2:00 PM – 6:00 PM Football practice

6:30 PM – 8:00 PM Mandatory study hall

After that, I had time to do more homework, go to bed, wake up and do it all over again. I was struggling mentally because I was far away from home. I didn't have many friends on the team, my coaches didn't like me, and my girlfriend cheated on me. There came a point when I felt like my decisions really didn't matter anymore. Nothing worked and I was feeling low, so I wanted to get high.

By Spring Break, I had enough and when I got home, I decided I was going to smoke some weed to help me feel better. And it worked…. at first, I felt relief but then the reality of my decision kicked in. The very first day back at school I faced a 6:03 AM drug test. So many thoughts were running rapidly through my mind. Are they going to pick me? Am I getting kicked off the team? Will my parents find out? Am I going to lose my scholarship? Was it worth it?

Then they called my name 'Tre' Gammage' the weight of the world now on my shoulders. I've worked so hard to get to this point, blood, sweat and tears. Now it might be gone because I chose a temporary relief of my pain. When it feels like your decisions matter the least, they count the most. It matters the most when you fight instead of walking away, stay quiet instead of speaking up, tell a lie versus the truth, making a wrong decision when you know what's right. In this case I was fortunate not to lose my scholarship. It was my first offense, so I received a warning, a conversation with my parents, and sessions with the psychologist. My Coach Baldy sat me down after everything happened taught me about The Dash.

Every Decision Counts

Baldy explained, "The dash is the small line between the day you were born, and the day you pass away. You will be remembered for what happens in your dash, it's your legacy, your decisions, and what you leave behind for those you love." The dash is where you find out life is All about you and at the same time Not about you.

It's all about you because the only part of life you can control is the decisions you make every day. You have to choose to be happy, you choose to put in the work, you choose to be a good friend and make good decisions.

"The easiest thing to find on God's green earth is someone to tell you all the things you cannot do" -Richard Devo's

It's easy for your class to not like you. It's easy for people to talk behind your back. People love to hate, but you can't control that. In college I let the haters get in my head. I wasn't forced to make a bad decision; I chose to make a decision that could have changed the direction of my life.

Have you made a decision you wish you could take back?

While you can't change what happened in the past, you can decide what comes next. When you are surrounded by only quality people your decisions will make a positive difference.

On the other side, life is not about you. You were born to help others. Some people were born to change the world, others were born to help family, friends, and animals. What you are meant to do in life is much bigger than you. So yes, you have to make every decision count because you are the only one in control of your life. But if you are selfish in your decision making, you can end up with your childhood dream in someone else's hands. Success is all about you, but it's not enough. When you are successful you have done something for yourself. When you become significant you are helping others.

The Nobel Peace Prize

One of the most prestigious awards in the world is the Nobel Peace prize. People like Nelson Mandela, Barack Obama, Martin Luther King Jr. have won this award. The award was founded by Alfred Nobel in 1895, a famous scientist, inventor and businessman born in Sweden. However, Alfred was first known for his experiment with mixing a chemical paste that could be shaped into rods, that came to be known as dynamite' in 1867.

At first people mining for diamonds and searching for gold used dynamite. But after a while people started using dynamite in the War as bombs that would destroy anything in its path. Well Alfred's brother Ludwig passed away, but the newspaper made a mistake and wrote an obituary for Alfred. They called him the 'Merchant of death' because he made it possible to destroy entire armies with the push of a button. When Alfred read this, he was disgusted with how people thought of him. It was a warning; he spent a lifetime creating ways to harm people. So, in 1895 Alfred decided he wanted to leave a new legacy and be remembered for something more peaceful. Alfred took his fortune worth over $186 million in today's money and used it to fund the Five Nobel Prizes.

While you can't change what happened in your past you can decide what comes next.

Reflection

1. Have you ever made a decision you wish you could take back? What happened? What lesson did you learn? What would you do different if you had to go through it again?

_____
_____
_____
_____

2. Growing up playing football in college was my dream, what's yours? Are you on the right track? How do you know?

_____
_____
_____
_____

3. What stood out to you in this chapter and why?

_____
_____
_____
_____

Chapter 6

Praising Insecurities

Haters are going to hate. Truthfully, it's not because they don't believe in you, but they don't believe in themselves. What is making you feel insecure today, is what makes you unique. You aren't supposed to be like anyone else.

Growing up, Ashley Varner was taller than all the boys and girls in her class, so she always felt awkward. Classmates constantly bashed her body calling her too skinny, lanky, awkward, too tall, no butt, and flat chested.

Have you felt like this before? Listening to your classmates constantly talking about you for parts of your life you can't control. It can make you want to hide from your insecurities and vulnerabilities. This body shaming went on for years until Ashley started playing basketball. Hooping was her outlet. When you play sports it's about being competitive and building relationships not what you look like. You have to learn to love the challenge.

While Ashley's outlet was basketball, her real dream was to rip the runway. Looking forward to an aspiring career Ashley placed lofty goals in front of her. She wanted to model on the biggest fashion stages, LA Fashion week, Nike, Paul Mitchell, and the international stages. The goal was set but the thoughts of being too tall, not pretty enough, and awkward were still playing on a loop in her mind until she read this quote:

"You are imperfect, permanently and inevitably flawed and you are beautiful because of it."

It was during a photo shoot that the way she posed and everything about her stood out perfectly. The physical features that classmates used to laugh at turned into a dream come true.

You are the only you there is, no one else is like you. We live in a time when you want to look like someone else instead of being who you are. Being a model isn't all about looks, the main thing you are bringing to the table as a model is being yourself.

Pain is Purpose

It's amazing how the situations that cause you the most pain are the same situations that help you grow. But before you can grow from your pain or situation you have to accept what happened as the truth. When you acknowledge what happened you can let it go and move on. You don't get to choose what family you are born into, how many parents are at home, what you look like, these are elements of your story, but your situation doesn't define who you are.

Insecurity: lack of confidence in yourself

List three areas that you feel a lack of self-confidence or doubt in yourself?

1. _____

2. _____

3. _____

Find at least 3 people, and talk with them about areas that you feel insecure, and brainstorm how you can turn your insecurities into a strength or advantage?

1. _____

2. _____

3. _____

Think forward, how do you see these insecurities becoming benefits as you grow older?

_____

_____

_____

Part 3 Released Expectations

A lot of people like to give different effort in different situations. But if you gave the same effort all the time and didn't worry about someone else's expectations of you what would be different? Try, giving the same effort in everything you do and the world's opportunities will start to open up to you.

Chapter 7

Released Expectations

When you let go of other people's expectations, what other people see as failure, you'll start to see as opportunity. Growing up I was an only child living with my Mom. I remember when I was 5 my Mom woke me up in the middle of the night in a panic "Tre', Tre' wake up it's time to go." She started stuffing a trash bag with clothes. I saw her count $300, we got in the car and pulled off. We just drove, until we got to Indianapolis, Indiana and went to a hotel that let us stay a couple nights for free. Eventually, we found an apartment with the first month's rent free and met a wealthy family that lived in a huge mansion. They needed a nanny, so my Mom helped raise their kids and keep the house in top shape. We stayed for two years.

It wasn't until 19 years later when I was 24 year's old that I asked about the whole story. When we left the house that night, her boyfriend had been holding her at gunpoint and told her she couldn't leave. It was an abusive relationship that we had to get away from. At the same time, I was preparing to compete in an International speech competition. The Toastmasters World Championship of Public Speaking. There are 143 countries, and 30,000 contestant's that enter the competition each year.

We started with a local competition and then moved up to statewide. After I won the South Carolina championship, I was a part of the Top 100 speakers in the world! It might sound crazy, but I told the story about leaving home in the middle of the night. Once I was able to talk out loud about my past, I was able to let it go, and move on.

This was a situation I was born into, but it was not a situation that I would let define my life.

The Story You're Afraid to Tell

When you let go of expectations, the world has a way of showing you endless opportunities. And believe me, there's an expectation for everything, your homework assignments, how to clean your room, what your friends think about you. I won't lie to you, I've been afraid to tell the full story of my childhood because I didn't want anyone to look at me differently.

Released Expectations

My friend Josephine Lee is literally a Top 3 public speaker in the world. In 2016 Josephine, myself and 30,000 contestants decided to compete for the title World Champion of Public Speaking. This is an intense global six round competition with speakers from 143 countries. As soon as I heard about the competition, I knew that I would be the #1 speaker in the world! If you had 5 – 7 minutes to say anything you wanted to the world what would it be? That's what this competition was like.

Every Decision Counts

During each of the six rounds competition stiffens. In South Carolina, (where I live) the state championship round would determine who was going to Washington DC to compete against the top 100 speakers in the world. It was a close contest but fortunately I pulled out the victory. You know me by now, I'm a former athlete so competition is my thing. On August 2, 2016, all of the remaining 100 contestants and representatives from 143 countries made the journey to Washington DC for the Semi Finals and Finals. My Semifinal round included the Champion speaker of Mexico, Turkey, Japan, Ohio, Louisiana, New York and more. I was locked in, ready to blow the world out of the water. In sports when you compete against another team you aren't supposed to like them until the game is over. But this competition wasn't the same, there wasn't a team I was competing against there was only myself. If I didn't go give my best speech, then it wouldn't matter if I was better than anyone else.

Before our semifinal round, everyone was so friendly. People were sharing headphones, dancing together, and enjoying the world stage. Maybe I was just nervous because I had to go first! Nobody likes going first, the crowd wasn't warmed up, nobody was ready to laugh. My story was pretty intense, my first line was 'all it takes is one decision, to change the direction of your life and when I was 20, I made a decision that I wanted to take back.'

It was an excellent speech well performed, but I knew as soon as I stepped off the stage that it wouldn't be enough to win. As the rest of the contestants began to take the stage, I sat in the front row sulking, until I started to recognize how powerful everyone's speech was.

It was a tough group! Then I didn't feel so bad, I did my part, and even if I didn't win, I learned that it's not all about me.

Success vs Significance

After the competition, I learned more about Josephine and her business. She's a ballerina by trade who opened 'The Pointe Shop' a one-stop shop for all your dancing needs. A successful venture, dancers were traveling up to 3 hours to come get fitted for their pointe shoes. But there wasn't a lot of opportunity for growth, so Josephine and her team had a radical idea. Get rid of everything else, leotards, tights, dresses, accessories shirts, all of it and focus only on fitting ballerinas for their shoes.

Instead of working out of a brick and mortar dance shop, they bought a van stuffed it full of shoes, and started traveling the country. People like specialties, ballet messes up your feet, so you want to make sure you are fitted right for minimal damage. The Pointe Shop is now the only pointe fitting shoe company in the country. The ultimate goal is to have a fitter in every major city in the country. She was even featured on Lifetime Network's version of Shark Tank: 'Project Runway: Fashion Start Up.'

Josephine told me, "Everybody should have a purpose. Pointe shoes are a vehicle to help make the world a better place."

When she made the transition from selling everything to selling one thing nobody thought it was a good idea. They gave up 80% of their inventory (everything they sell), which also meant they lost 80% of revenue (how much money comes in every year). It was a bold move to change from a successful company to a significant business. But it was worth it. It happened because she understood that when you let go of expectations the world opens up to you and there are endless opportunities.

Reflection

Where have you had the most success so far in life? School, sports, music, art, making friends, something else. (see ch 4. 'What are you're the best at)

_____
_____
_____
_____

Is there an expectation holding you back from being even better? It could be a parent, teacher, friend, or your own mind.

_____
_____
_____
_____

What would happen in your life if you let go of the expectations other people have for you?

_____
_____
_____
_____

Chapter 8

What's Growing in Your Garden?

Your mind is like a garden. You must tend to the weeds and plant the seeds. When you set goals, your focus isn't about the reward at the end of the journey. It's about being the person you need to be to make that dream a reality. What's growing in your garden? Do you think negative thoughts? Negative thoughts are like weeds, they grow by themselves. It's easy to wake up in the morning and not want to get out of bed, doubt yourself, or just not feel like doing anything. So, you have the task of planting more seeds in your garden so you can cultivate your mind and receive the harvest that you've planted. Even if you are excited about where you are there's a higher platform for you to reach. It's your job to cultivate your mind and pull up the weeds.

Every season is different. What got you here, won't get you there. How do you cultivate your garden? Keep reading to find out.

Plant More Seeds

Flowers don't grow by themselves. You have to dig the hole, plant the seed, water it, and wait for it to grow. Muhammad Ali said that everything good that God made we have to look for. Mine for gold, dig for diamonds, search for what you want. What do you want growing in your garden and how many seeds do you need to plant to get there?

The question overall is bigger than 'what do I get'. It's more like 'who do I have to become to achieve the goal'. Forget about the reward for a minute and think about who it is you have to be. For you to reach your full potential, there are parts of you that have to change. What do you have to do to become who you want to be?

It starts with your daily bread. In 2016, I took a visit to Chicago and had a conversation with the Homeless Coalition. While there, I met Stefano. His father was actually a King Pin in Pablo Escobar's drug cartel, so his dad wasn't really around. His journey through childhood was difficult. At five, he was sexually abused by his stepfather. At age 10, he was diagnosed with Bipolar personality disorder and ultimately ended up turning to drugs. By 18, he was homeless sleeping under a bridge, went to jail, and at 6 feet tall he weighed 90 pounds. Stefano shared how he continued to turn to drugs and alcohol. Though he wanted to stop, he couldn't change until he decided he had enough. He wasn't at all what I thought to be a homeless person. He'd been through much, so I asked him, "How do you live with Bipolar Disorder and cope with what you've been through?" He responded, "Every day is a new challenge. I wake up and start over."

Daily bread: Have you ever tried a morning routine? You probably still don't like getting up in the morning.

It would be different if you had a morning routine. Just take 15 minutes to thrive and set your day up for success.

Here's my routine…

Pray

Read my Bible

Write in my journal

Plan and set goals for the day

You can exchange any step of my routine, with whatever works for you. Remember, in Chapter 4 we talked about victory loving preparation. When you start your day off with a consistent routine, you are pulling the weeds out of your garden and choosing positive thoughts to start your day.

Keep Up the Maintenance

Keep doing the little things right. Go to bed on time. Wake up on time. Keep following your routine. I know you've seen a garden without a caretaker. Weeds will sprout over 6 feet tall; bugs start to eat all your flowers. It will start to look really bad. When you see a well-kept garden, one that someone tends to daily, it's in much better shape. Everything is in order. The flowers blossom, and the seeds grow.

You are still going to have bad days. There will be days you'll want to sleep in and not do anything. That's just fine. It's ok to reset and then get back to it. When you feel stuck, reach out for help. You don't have to do it alone. Have somebody that's not going to tell you want to hear, but someone that's going to help you push forward. Reach out and you'll be surprised at the help you get in return.

Find a Buddy

Do you know the story of the praying hands? They're probably the most famous hands in the world. Albrecht Durer was born in the time of Nazi Germany. He was one of eighteen children. Albrecht and his twin brother had a desire to do something great for their family. The only way they would make it out of Germany was doing it together. They flipped a coin. One brother, Albert, would work in a mine while Albrecht went to Art school. By the time Albrecht finished school, he was commanding top dollar for his work and it was time for the brothers to switch roles. However, Albert's hands were too beaten and broken from working in the mine to still be an artist. Albrecht was so sad about this because they made a deal. The decision Albert made to support Albrecht ultimately cost him his opportunity to be an Artist. Howevet, he also gave Albrecht the opportunity to see their dream become a reality. To honor Albert's sacrifice, Albrecht create the Praying Hands painting that's known around the world.

Albert and Albrecht weren't just brothers, they were partners. Find a buddy to help you cultivate your mind, someone to help you stay strong when you are feeling down.

Cultivate Your Garden

Planting seeds in your mind's garden is the same as setting goals. What you think about the most is what is going to become your reality. If you don't know what you want, you don't know what you'll get. If you know exactly what you want, you'll know exactly what to expect.

Goal: There are short-term goals, long-term goals, and Lifetime goals (they take forever). If you haven't set goals before here's your chance.

Short term goals: Set a goal for what you would like to achieve over the next month.

Family: _____

Friends: _____

School: _____

Other: _____

Long term goals: Set a goal that you would like to achieve in the next 6 months.

Family: _____

Friends: _____

School: _____

Other: _____

Your goals should be SMARTIES

Specific – make them detailed and specific as possible

Measurable – Make sure you are able to measure whether you reach the goal

As if now – Write your goals in the present tense like it's already happened

Timebound – Put a timeframe on when you would like to achieve the goal

Interesting – Make your goals about things that you find interesting and worthwhile

Emotional – Use powerful language to express the emotion behind the goals

Success oriented – express your goals in a success focused way

Action & Routine: List 5 actions you can take to achieve your goal and when you will do them.

1. _____
2. _____
3. _____
4. _____
5. _____

Accountability Partner: Explain how you will remind yourself to take action on these goals.

_____
_____
_____
_____
_____

Tre' Gammage

www.ingramcontent.com/pod-product-compliance
Lightning Source LLC
Chambersburg PA
CBHW052120070526
44584CB00017B/2570